QURAN
50 VITAL VERSES

Shaykh Fadhlalla Haeri

Publisher: Zahra Publications
ISBN: 978-1-919826-97-4
Typeset by: Mizpah Marketing Concepts
Cover design by: Kim Gaul - Jump Monkey

http://www.sfhfoundation.com
www.zahrapublications.com
© Zahra Publications

All rights reserved. Except for brief quotations in critical articles or reviews, no part of this book may be reproduced in any manner without prior written permission from Zahra Publications.

Contents

Reality — 7

Creation — 23

Realities — 41

Humans — 59

Two Lives — 79

Eternity — 99

Notes — 119

This book was compiled and produced by the late Hashim Ismail under the supervision of Shaykh Fadhlalla Haeri.

It is dedicated to his memory.

Introduction

Human beings always quest for a better life. What is it? Where, when and how can it be found? The Qur'an is an interactive manual for achieveing this wholesome living. It sketches for us, different facets and levels of realities emanating from the one Real, demonstrating their interconnectedness and original Oneness. It also prescribes pathways of conduct and relationships that enhance earthly life and lead to an appropriate destiny.

Our Earthly life is a connector between the limited visible and the infinite unseen. We are alive due to a mysterious light within our heart, often referred to as the soul or spirit. Our physical body and mind have evolved from inert matter into a complex system that is alive with consciousness. Our humanity is the home of divinity, and as such, our duty and destiny are to experience this truth and celebrate perpetual Reality. We are short-term guests on earth, and will only enjoy our stay once we are in constant awareness of the timelessness of our soul, the resident master and link to Allah. This *dhikr* or awareness will lead us to the perfect destiny.

At all times, human beings are at a loss. Awakening to truth changes our self-inflicted tragedies to absurd comedies; that is the light emanating from the lens of Oneness – Allah. We shall die and our borrowed identity will return to higher Reality. Experiencing the lights and delights of the soul whilst on earth is a rehearsal of the state described as paradise. Through living faith, trust, selflessness and dedicated action with others on the same path, we can calibrate and balance our life between human consciousness and emotion to the timeless spiritual reality of our soul. A perfect destiny.

I am grateful to the discernable and invisible grace of Allah that perpetuates the Universe. I would like to thank Muneera Haeri, Leyya Kalla, Ahmed Sheriff and other friends and supporters.

Shaykh Fadhlalla Haeri

March 2015

Reality

اللَّهُ نُورُ السَّمَاوَاتِ وَالْأَرْضِ ۚ مَثَلُ نُورِهِ كَمِشْكَاةٍ فِيهَا مِصْبَاحٌ ۖ الْمِصْبَاحُ فِي زُجَاجَةٍ ۖ الزُّجَاجَةُ كَأَنَّهَا كَوْكَبٌ دُرِّيٌّ يُوقَدُ مِنْ شَجَرَةٍ مُبَارَكَةٍ زَيْتُونَةٍ لَا شَرْقِيَّةٍ وَلَا غَرْبِيَّةٍ يَكَادُ زَيْتُهَا يُضِيءُ وَلَوْ لَمْ تَمْسَسْهُ نَارٌ ۚ نُورٌ عَلَىٰ نُورٍ ۗ يَهْدِي اللَّهُ لِنُورِهِ مَنْ يَشَاءُ ۚ وَيَضْرِبُ اللَّهُ الْأَمْثَالَ لِلنَّاسِ ۗ وَاللَّهُ بِكُلِّ شَيْءٍ عَلِيمٌ 24:35

Allah is the Light of the heavens and the earth. The Parable of His Light is as if there were a Niche and within it a Lamp: the Lamp enclosed in Glass: the glass as it were a brilliant star: Lit from a blessed Tree, an Olive, neither of the east nor of the west, whose oil is well-nigh luminous, though fire scarce touched it: Light upon Light! Allah doth guide whom He will to His Light: Allah doth set forth Parables for men: and Allah doth know all things. 24:35

Reality

Light and energy are vast in varieties and types. The light package within the human heart or soul is one representation.

إِنَّ اللَّهَ لَهُ مُلْكُ السَّمَاوَاتِ وَالْأَرْضِ ۖ يُحْيِي وَيُمِيتُ ۚ وَمَا لَكُم مِّن دُونِ اللَّهِ مِن وَلِيٍّ وَلَا نَصِيرٍ 9:116

Unto Allah belongeth the dominion of the heavens and the earth. He giveth life and He taketh it. Except for Him ye have no protector nor helper. 9:116

Reality

*The universe is governed and held
by Allah's Reality.*

هُوَ الْأَوَّلُ وَالْآخِرُ وَالظَّاهِرُ وَالْبَاطِنُ ۖ وَهُوَ بِكُلِّ شَيْءٍ عَلِيمٌ 57:3

He is the First and the Last, the Evident and the Immanent: and He has full knowledge of all things.
57:3

Reality

*Reality, Allah, is before beginnings and
after ends; both evident and hidden.
Cosmic consciousness envelops all.*

وَتَرَى الْجِبَالَ تَحْسَبُهَا جَامِدَةً وَهِيَ تَمُرُّ مَرَّ السَّحَابِ ۚ صُنْعَ اللَّهِ الَّذِي أَتْقَنَ كُلَّ شَيْءٍ ۚ إِنَّهُ خَبِيرٌ بِمَا تَفْعَلُونَ 27:88

Thou seest the mountains and thinkest them firmly fixed: but they shall pass away as the clouds pass away: (such is) the artistry of Allah, who disposes of all things in perfect order: for he is well acquainted with all that ye do. 27:88

Reality

What appears solid and massive is in fact moving swiftly towards its destiny, Nothingness.

أَلَمْ تَرَ أَنَّ اللَّهَ يَعْلَمُ مَا فِي السَّمَاوَاتِ وَمَا فِي الْأَرْضِ ۖ مَا يَكُونُ مِنْ نَجْوَىٰ ثَلَاثَةٍ إِلَّا هُوَ رَابِعُهُمْ وَلَا خَمْسَةٍ إِلَّا هُوَ سَادِسُهُمْ وَلَا أَدْنَىٰ مِنْ ذَٰلِكَ وَلَا أَكْثَرَ إِلَّا هُوَ مَعَهُمْ أَيْنَ مَا كَانُوا ۖ ثُمَّ يُنَبِّئُهُمْ بِمَا عَمِلُوا يَوْمَ الْقِيَامَةِ ۚ إِنَّ اللَّهَ بِكُلِّ شَيْءٍ عَلِيمٌ 58:7

Seest thou not that Allah doth know (all) that
is in the heavens and on earth? There is not
a secret consultation between three, but He
makes the fourth among them, - Nor between
five but He makes the sixth,- nor between fewer
nor more, but He is in their midst, wheresoever
they be: In the end will He tell them the truth
of their conduct, on the Day of Judgment.
For Allah has full knowledge of all things. 58:7

Reality

Allah's light permeates everything and at all times. If we do not perceive it now it will be evident in the hereafter.

وَلَقَدْ خَلَقْنَا الْإِنْسَانَ وَنَعْلَمُ مَا تُوَسْوِسُ بِهِ نَفْسُهُ وَنَحْنُ أَقْرَبُ إِلَيْهِ مِنْ حَبْلِ الْوَرِيدِ 50:16

It was We Who created man, and We know what dark suggestions his soul makes to him: for We are nearer to him than (his) jugular vein. 50:16

Reality

*Humans are gripped within every cell
by the light of Allah.*

$$\text{وَلِلَّهِ الْمَشْرِقُ وَالْمَغْرِبُ ۚ فَأَيْنَمَا تُوَلُّوا فَثَمَّ وَجْهُ اللَّهِ ۚ إِنَّ اللَّهَ وَاسِعٌ عَلِيمٌ}\ \text{2:115}$$

To Allah belong the east and the West: Whithersoever ye turn, there is the presence of Allah. For Allah is all-Pervading, all-Knowing. 2:115

Reality

And to Allah belongs whatever is within space and time – the Vast All-Knowing.

Creation

وَمِنْ كُلِّ شَيْءٍ خَلَقْنَا زَوْجَيْنِ لَعَلَّكُمْ تَذَكَّرُونَ 51:49

And of every thing We have created pairs: That ye may receive instruction. 51:49

Creation

*Existence is balanced by the two sides
of Oneness. Reflection upon this saves
us from affliction.*

وَمَا خَلَقْتُ الْجِنَّ وَالْإِنْسَ إِلَّا لِيَعْبُدُونِ 51:56

I have only created Jinns and men, that they may serve Me. 51:56

Creation

You worship what you love and are obsessed with. Perfect destiny is to live by the soul and to unify with it, the ultimate worship.

وَيَسْتَعْجِلُونَكَ بِالْعَذَابِ وَلَنْ يُخْلِفَ اللَّهُ وَعْدَهُ ۚ وَإِنَّ يَوْمًا عِندَ رَبِّكَ كَأَلْفِ سَنَةٍ مِّمَّا تَعُدُّونَ 22:47

Yet they ask thee to hasten on the Punishment! But Allah will not fail in His Promise. Verily a Day in the sight of thy Lord is like a thousand years of your reckoning. 22:47

Creation

It is natural to be in a rush, yet the soul is timeless. A thousand years of human measure is like one day with the Creator. Time is a relative illusion framed by space.

خَلَقَ السَّمَاوَاتِ وَالْأَرْضَ بِالْحَقِّ ۖ يُكَوِّرُ اللَّيْلَ عَلَى النَّهَارِ وَيُكَوِّرُ النَّهَارَ عَلَى اللَّيْلِ ۖ وَسَخَّرَ الشَّمْسَ وَالْقَمَرَ ۖ كُلٌّ يَجْرِي لِأَجَلٍ مُسَمًّى ۗ أَلَا هُوَ الْعَزِيزُ الْغَفَّارُ 39:5

He created the heavens and the earth in true (proportions): He makes the Night overlap the Day, and the Day overlap the Night: He has subjected the sun and the moon (to His law): Each one follows a course for a time appointed. Is not He the Exalted in Power - He Who forgives again and again? 39:5

Creation

*All emanates from truth and carries a spark
of it, but the appearances vary in light
and darkness according to the drift of time.*

كَانَ النَّاسُ أُمَّةً وَاحِدَةً فَبَعَثَ اللَّهُ النَّبِيِّينَ مُبَشِّرِينَ وَمُنْذِرِينَ وَأَنْزَلَ مَعَهُمُ الْكِتَابَ بِالْحَقِّ لِيَحْكُمَ بَيْنَ النَّاسِ فِيمَا اخْتَلَفُوا فِيهِ ۚ وَمَا اخْتَلَفَ فِيهِ إِلَّا الَّذِينَ أُوتُوهُ مِنْ بَعْدِ مَا جَاءَتْهُمُ الْبَيِّنَاتُ بَغْيًا بَيْنَهُمْ ۖ فَهَدَى اللَّهُ الَّذِينَ آمَنُوا لِمَا اخْتَلَفُوا فِيهِ مِنَ الْحَقِّ بِإِذْنِهِ ۗ وَاللَّهُ يَهْدِي مَنْ يَشَاءُ إِلَىٰ صِرَاطٍ مُسْتَقِيمٍ 2:213

Mankind was one single nation, and Allah sent Messengers with glad tidings and warnings; and with them He sent the Book in truth, to judge between people in matters wherein they differed; but the People of the Book, after the clear Signs came to them, did not differ among themselves, except through selfish contumacy. Allah by His Grace Guided the believers to the Truth, concerning that wherein they differed. For Allah guided whom He will to a path that is straight. 2:213

Creation

Humans emanated from One source and then spread out as clans and groups towards the same quested destiny, to realise divine presence.

الَّذِي خَلَقَ الْمَوْتَ وَالْحَيَاةَ لِيَبْلُوَكُمْ أَيُّكُمْ أَحْسَنُ عَمَلًا وَهُوَ الْعَزِيزُ الْغَفُورُ 67:2

He Who created Death and Life, that He may try which of you is best in deed: and He is the Exalted in Might, Oft-Forgiving;- 67:2

Creation

The ultimate good action is that which reduces the self and veils the ego. Life leads to living as a divine spark, as a soul. This is the main task for humanity.

وَهُوَ الَّذِي أَنْشَأَكُمْ مِنْ نَفْسٍ وَاحِدَةٍ فَمُسْتَقَرٌّ وَمُسْتَوْدَعٌ ۗ قَدْ فَصَّلْنَا الْآيَاتِ لِقَوْمٍ يَفْقَهُونَ 6:98

It is He Who hath produced you from a single person: here is a place of sojourn and a place of departure: We detail Our signs for people who understand. 6:98

Creation

Physics and metaphysics are signs that can lead to spiritual awakening. All human souls are the same. Humans only differ according to the lower self and the extent of its darkness upon the soul.

تُسَبِّحُ لَهُ السَّمَاوَاتُ السَّبْعُ وَالْأَرْضُ وَمَن فِيهِنَّ ۚ وَإِن مِّن شَيْءٍ إِلَّا يُسَبِّحُ بِحَمْدِهِ وَلَٰكِن لَّا تَفْقَهُونَ تَسْبِيحَهُمْ ۗ إِنَّهُ كَانَ حَلِيمًا غَفُورًا 17:44

The seven heavens and the earth, and all beings therein, declare His glory: there is not a thing but celebrates His praise; And yet ye understand not how they declare His glory! Verily He is Oft-Forbear, Most Forgiving! 17:44

Creation

The Universe is held by the powers of connectedness through qualities and attributes. Existence relates to connectedness and continuation, flavoured by a desirable quality or direction.

Realities

وَفِي الْأَرْضِ آيَاتٌ لِلْمُوقِنِينَ 51:20

On the earth are signs for those of assured Faith, 51:20

وَفِي أَنفُسِكُمْ ۚ أَفَلَا تُبْصِرُونَ 51:21

As also in your own selves: Will ye not then see? 51:21

وَفِي السَّمَاءِ رِزْقُكُمْ وَمَا تُوعَدُونَ 51:22

And in heaven is your Sustenance, as (also) that which ye are promised. 51:22

Realities

Universal interconnectedness permeates all levels and states. Through deep contemplation, we can discern the seamless relation between the visible and invisible.

وَنَفْسٍ وَمَا سَوَّاهَا

فَأَلْهَمَهَا فُجُورَهَا وَتَقْوَاهَا 91:7-8

By the Soul, and the proportion and order given to it;

And its enlightenment as to its wrong and its right;-
91:7-8

Realities

The self is alive due to the soul but relates mostly to body and mind. On one side it is light and delight. On the other side it is decay and fear.

وَكُلُّ شَيْءٍ فَعَلُوهُ فِي الزُّبُرِ

وَكُلُّ صَغِيرٍ وَكَبِيرٍ مُسْتَطَرٌ 54:52-53

All that they do is noted in (their) Books (of Deeds):

Every matter, small and great, is on record. 54:52-53

Realities

Nothing in existence can occur without a beginning and an end, leaving its trace and story behind.

قُلْ لَا أَمْلِكُ لِنَفْسِي نَفْعًا وَلَا ضَرًّا إِلَّا مَا شَاءَ اللَّهُ ۚ وَلَوْ كُنتُ أَعْلَمُ الْغَيْبَ لَاسْتَكْثَرْتُ مِنَ الْخَيْرِ وَمَا مَسَّنِيَ السُّوءُ ۚ إِنْ أَنَا إِلَّا نَذِيرٌ وَبَشِيرٌ لِقَوْمٍ يُؤْمِنُونَ

7:188

Say: "I have no power over any good or harm to myself except as Allah willeth. If I had knowledge of the unseen, I should have multiplied all good, and no evil should have touched me: I am but a warner, and a bringer of glad tidings to those who have faith." 7:188

Realities

*Allah is the source of all powers and lights.
We are led according to our potential and
willingness towards the light of lights.
Faith and trust open the door.*

قُلْ لَوْ كَانَ الْبَحْرُ مِدَادًا لِكَلِمَاتِ رَبِّي لَنَفِدَ الْبَحْرُ قَبْلَ أَنْ تَنْفَدَ كَلِمَاتُ رَبِّي وَلَوْ جِئْنَا بِمِثْلِهِ مَدَدًا 18:109

Say: "If the ocean were ink (wherewith to write out) the words of my Lord, sooner would the ocean be exhausted than would the words of my Lord, even if we added another ocean like it, for its aid." 18:109

Realities

*Creational possibilities are infinite;
every possible combination within time
and space is possible.*

وَمَا نُرِيهِم مِّنْ آيَةٍ إِلَّا هِيَ أَكْبَرُ مِنْ أُخْتِهَا ۖ وَأَخَذْنَاهُم بِالْعَذَابِ لَعَلَّهُمْ يَرْجِعُونَ 43:48

We showed them Sign after Sign, each greater than its fellow, and We seized them with Punishment, in order that they might turn (to Us). 43:48

Realities

*We are explorers of knowledge and insights.
Evolution is moving towards higher
consciousness, back to the origin of all being.*

كُلُّ نَفْسٍ ذَائِقَةُ الْمَوْتِ ۗ وَنَبْلُوكُم بِالشَّرِّ وَالْخَيْرِ فِتْنَةً ۖ وَإِلَيْنَا تُرْجَعُونَ 21:35

Every soul shall have a taste of death: and We test you by evil and by good by way of trial. to Us must ye return. 21:35

Realities

For the awakened being, life is continuous, and tasting death is part of earthly experience; so is the interplay of good and bad, day and night.

يَا أَيُّهَا النَّاسُ اتَّقُوا رَبَّكُمْ وَاخْشَوْا يَوْمًا لَا يَجْزِي وَالِدٌ عَنْ وَلَدِهِ وَلَا مَوْلُودٌ هُوَ جَازٍ عَنْ وَالِدِهِ شَيْئًا ۚ إِنَّ وَعْدَ اللَّهِ حَقٌّ ۖ فَلَا تَغُرَّنَّكُمُ الْحَيَاةُ الدُّنْيَا وَلَا يَغُرَّنَّكُم بِاللَّهِ الْغَرُورُ 31:33

O mankind! do your duty to your Lord, and fear (the coming of) a Day when no father can avail aught for his son, nor a son avail aught for his father. Verily, the promise of Allah is true: let not then this present life deceive you, nor let the chief Deceiver deceive you about Allah. 31:33

Realities

*During life on earth, we have a
certain measure of freedom of action.
Disempowerment prevails after death and all
that is left is the soul's energy and experience
whilst on earth. The less the darkness of the
self the greater the light of the soul.*

Humans

وَعَلَّمَ آدَمَ الْأَسْمَاءَ كُلَّهَا ثُمَّ عَرَضَهُمْ عَلَى الْمَلَائِكَةِ فَقَالَ أَنْبِئُونِي بِأَسْمَاءِ هَؤُلَاءِ إِنْ كُنْتُمْ صَادِقِينَ 2:31

And He taught Adam the names of all things; then He placed them before the angels, and said: "Tell me the names of these if ye are right." 2:31

Humans

The soul of Adam was illumined by knowledge of all realities and potential entities. Our journey is from outer entities to the ultimate inner lights and patterns.

وَلَنَبْلُوَنَّكُم بِشَيْءٍ مِنَ الْخَوْفِ وَالْجُوعِ وَنَقْصٍ مِنَ الْأَمْوَالِ وَالْأَنفُسِ وَالثَّمَرَاتِ ۗ وَبَشِّرِ الصَّابِرِينَ 2:155

Be sure we shall test you with something of fear and hunger, some loss in goods or lives or the fruits (of your toil), but give glad tidings to those who patiently persevere, 2:155

Humans

All our experiences are balanced between attraction and repulsion. Liberation from these dualities is through the experience of the inner light, which can only happen when we transcend the limitations of time.

وَإِذْ نَتَقْنَا الْجَبَلَ فَوْقَهُمْ كَأَنَّهُ ظُلَّةٌ وَظَنُّوا أَنَّهُ وَاقِعٌ بِهِمْ خُذُوا مَا آتَيْنَاكُم بِقُوَّةٍ وَاذْكُرُوا مَا فِيهِ لَعَلَّكُمْ تَتَّقُونَ

7:171

When We shook the Mount over them, as if it had been a canopy, and they thought it was going to fall on them (We said): "Hold firmly to what We have given you, and bring (ever) to remembrance what is therein; perchance ye may fear Allah." 7:171

Humans

The package that leads us to awakening is a complete and integrated one that must be taken in its totality. We cannot take parts of the Qur'an as and when it suits us.

يَا أَيُّهَا الَّذِينَ آمَنُوا اسْتَجِيبُوا لِلَّهِ وَلِلرَّسُولِ إِذَا دَعَاكُمْ لِمَا يُحْيِيكُمْ ۖ وَاعْلَمُوا أَنَّ اللَّهَ يَحُولُ بَيْنَ الْمَرْءِ وَقَلْبِهِ وَأَنَّهُ إِلَيْهِ تُحْشَرُونَ 8:24

O ye who believe! give your response to Allah and His Messenger, when He calleth you to that which will give you life; and know that Allah cometh in between a man and his heart, and that it is He to Whom ye shall (all) be gathered. 8:24

Humans

Personal life is a beam that emanates from the cosmic soul. In order to awaken to the cosmic soul, we need to transcend our self, mind and identity.

فَمَنْ يَعْمَلْ مِثْقَالَ ذَرَّةٍ خَيْرًا يَرَهُ

وَمَنْ يَعْمَلْ مِثْقَالَ ذَرَّةٍ شَرًّا يَرَهُ 99:7-8

Then shall anyone who has done an atom's weight of good, see it!

And anyone who has done an atom's weight of evil, shall see it. 99:7-8

Humans

*Our intentions or actions are never lost.
We shall face the consequences of all of these,
if not now then in the hereafter.*

مَا أَصَابَكَ مِنْ حَسَنَةٍ فَمِنَ اللَّهِ ۖ وَمَا أَصَابَكَ مِنْ سَيِّئَةٍ فَمِنْ نَفْسِكَ ۚ وَأَرْسَلْنَاكَ لِلنَّاسِ رَسُولًا ۚ وَكَفَىٰ بِاللَّهِ شَهِيدًا 4:79

Whatever good, (O man!) happens to thee, is from Allah; but whatever evil happens to thee, is from thy (own) soul. and We have sent thee as a messenger to (instruct) mankind. And enough is Allah for a witness. 4:79

Humans

The lower self is a veil and cover over the perfection that we aspire to. Most suffering is from the self, and all durable lights and delights are from the soul; Allah's agent.

قُلْ إِنْ كُنْتُمْ تُحِبُّونَ اللَّهَ فَاتَّبِعُونِي يُحْبِبْكُمُ اللَّهُ وَيَغْفِرْ لَكُمْ ذُنُوبَكُمْ ۗ وَاللَّهُ غَفُورٌ رَحِيمٌ 3:31

Say: If you love Allah, then follow me, Allah will love you and forgive you your faults, and Allah is Forgiving, Merciful. 3:31

*Love is the Universal glue that permeates
all of existence.*

*To unify with Allah, we need to follow
those truly absorbed in His light,
such as the Prophet.*

وَلَقَدْ عَلِمْتُمُ النَّشْأَةَ الْأُولَىٰ فَلَوْلَا تَذَكَّرُونَ 56:62

And ye certainly know already the first form of creation: why then do ye not celebrate His praises? 56:62

Humans

We have within us the seeds of our origin. When we go back in time to that point, we are at the beginning of all. Reflection takes us to the door of rising consciousness.

مَنْ جَاءَ بِالْحَسَنَةِ فَلَهُ عَشْرُ أَمْثَالِهَا ۖ وَمَنْ جَاءَ بِالسَّيِّئَةِ فَلَا يُجْزَىٰ إِلَّا مِثْلَهَا وَهُمْ لَا يُظْلَمُونَ 6:160

He that doeth good shall have ten times as much to his credit: He that doeth evil shall only be recompensed according to his evil: no wrong shall be done unto (any of) them. 6:160

Humans

To see through the lens of Oneness is the right path which was followed by all Prophets.

Two Lives

زُيِّنَ لِلَّذِينَ كَفَرُوا الْحَيَاةُ الدُّنْيَا وَيَسْخَرُونَ مِنَ الَّذِينَ آمَنُوا ۘ وَالَّذِينَ اتَّقَوْا فَوْقَهُمْ يَوْمَ الْقِيَامَةِ ۗ وَاللَّهُ يَرْزُقُ مَنْ يَشَاءُ بِغَيْرِ حِسَابٍ 2:212

The life of this world is alluring to those who reject faith, and they scoff at those who believe. But the righteous will be above them on the Day of Resurrection; for Allah bestows His abundance without measure on whom He will. 2:212

Two Lives

*Our Earthly life is attractive to the self.
Only through the soul's illumination can we
transcend it to the hereafter and its perpetuity.*

إِلَّا مَنْ تَابَ وَآمَنَ وَعَمِلَ عَمَلًا صَالِحًا فَأُولَٰئِكَ يُبَدِّلُ اللَّهُ سَيِّئَاتِهِمْ حَسَنَاتٍ ۗ وَكَانَ اللَّهُ غَفُورًا رَحِيمًا 25:70

Unless he repents, believes, and works righteous deeds, for Allah will change the evil of such persons into good, and Allah is Oft-Forgiving, Most Merciful, 25:70

Two Lives

We suffer from our wrong intentions and actions. Being more alert with our thoughts, speech and actions is the path of transcendence. Our life is a displacement of confusion with fusion.

كُتِبَ عَلَيْكُمُ الْقِتَالُ وَهُوَ كُرْهٌ لَكُمْ ۖ وَعَسَىٰ أَنْ تَكْرَهُوا شَيْئًا وَهُوَ خَيْرٌ لَكُمْ ۖ وَعَسَىٰ أَنْ تُحِبُّوا شَيْئًا وَهُوَ شَرٌّ لَكُمْ ۗ وَاللَّهُ يَعْلَمُ وَأَنْتُمْ لَا تَعْلَمُونَ 2:216

Fighting is prescribed for you, and ye dislike it. But it is possible that ye dislike a thing which is good for you, and that ye love a thing which is bad for you. But Allah knoweth, and ye know not. 2:216

Two Lives

The self has its likes and dislikes.
To evolve, we need to refer to
the soul rather than please the self.

أَفَلَمْ يَسِيرُوا فِي الْأَرْضِ فَتَكُونَ لَهُمْ قُلُوبٌ يَعْقِلُونَ بِهَا أَوْ آذَانٌ يَسْمَعُونَ بِهَا ۖ فَإِنَّهَا لَا تَعْمَى الْأَبْصَارُ وَلَٰكِن تَعْمَى الْقُلُوبُ الَّتِي فِي الصُّدُورِ 22:46

Do they not travel through the land, so that their hearts (and minds) may thus learn wisdom and their ears may thus learn to hear? Truly it is not their eyes that are blind, but their hearts which are in their breasts. 22:46

Two Lives

Everything is balanced between pluralities; our physical sight with insight, our mental comprehension with knowing by the heart. Sight is an outer manifestation of insight.

إِلَّا أَنْ يَشَاءَ اللَّهُ ۚ وَاذْكُرْ رَبَّكَ إِذَا نَسِيتَ وَقُلْ عَسَىٰ أَنْ يَهْدِيَنِ رَبِّي لِأَقْرَبَ مِنْ هَٰذَا رَشَدًا 18:24

Without adding, "So please Allah!" and call thy Lord to mind when thou forgettest, and say, "I hope that my Lord will guide me ever closer (even) than this to the right road." 18:24

Two Lives

Human nature is prone to forgetfulness. This can be the trigger point to remembrance and the reference back to the Maker of it all, whose presence is in the heart.

أَمَّنْ هُوَ قَانِتٌ آنَاءَ اللَّيْلِ سَاجِدًا وَقَائِمًا يَحْذَرُ الْآخِرَةَ وَيَرْجُو رَحْمَةَ رَبِّهِ ۗ قُلْ هَلْ يَسْتَوِي الَّذِينَ يَعْلَمُونَ وَالَّذِينَ لَا يَعْلَمُونَ ۗ إِنَّمَا يَتَذَكَّرُ أُولُو الْأَلْبَابِ 39:9

Is one who worships devoutly during the hour of the night prostrating himself or standing (in adoration), who takes heed of the Hereafter, and who places his hope in the Mercy of his Lord - (like one who does not)? Say: "Are those equal, those who know and those who do not know? It is those who are endued with understanding that receive admonition. 39:9

Two Lives

The more often you refer to your innermost, the more likely you are to be closer to the source of knowledge and awakening. What a difference between those who are asleep and those who are awake.

وَمَنْ كَانَ فِي هَٰذِهِ أَعْمَىٰ فَهُوَ فِي الْآخِرَةِ أَعْمَىٰ وَأَضَلُّ سَبِيلًا 17:72

But those who were blind in this world, will be blind in the hereafter, and most astray from the Path. 17:72

Two Lives

Worldly understanding, sight and comprehension are necessary steps towards illumination and experience of the hereafter, here and now.

هُوَ الَّذِي يُرِيكُمْ آيَاتِهِ وَيُنَزِّلُ لَكُمْ مِنَ السَّمَاءِ رِزْقًا ۚ وَمَا يَتَذَكَّرُ إِلَّا مَنْ يُنِيبُ 40:13

He it is Who showeth you his Signs, and sendeth down sustenance for you from the sky: but only those receive admonition who turn (to Allah). 40:13

Two Lives

Real meditation and reflection begin when we perceive our heavenly origin and take provision from that. Humanity will be completed by experiencing divinity within.

الْحَجُّ أَشْهُرٌ مَعْلُومَاتٌ ۚ فَمَنْ فَرَضَ فِيهِنَّ الْحَجَّ فَلَا رَفَثَ وَلَا فُسُوقَ وَلَا جِدَالَ فِي الْحَجِّ ۗ وَمَا تَفْعَلُوا مِنْ خَيْرٍ يَعْلَمْهُ اللَّهُ ۗ وَتَزَوَّدُوا فَإِنَّ خَيْرَ الزَّادِ التَّقْوَىٰ ۚ وَاتَّقُونِ يَا أُولِي الْأَلْبَابِ 2:197

For Hajj are the months well known. If any one undertakes that duty therein, Let there be no obscenity, nor wickedness, nor wrangling in the Hajj. And whatever good ye do, (be sure) Allah knoweth it. And take a provision (With you) for the journey, but the best of provisions is right conduct. So fear Me, o ye that are wise. 2:197

Two Lives

Those who reflect and are in God-awareness, must move along the path of higher intentions and actions.

Eternity

وَابْتَغِ فِيمَا آتَاكَ اللَّهُ الدَّارَ الْآخِرَةَ ۖ وَلَا تَنسَ نَصِيبَكَ مِنَ الدُّنْيَا ۖ وَأَحْسِن كَمَا أَحْسَنَ اللَّهُ إِلَيْكَ ۖ وَلَا تَبْغِ الْفَسَادَ فِي الْأَرْضِ ۖ إِنَّ اللَّهَ لَا يُحِبُّ الْمُفْسِدِينَ 28:77

"But seek, with the (wealth) which Allah has bestowed on thee, the Home of the Hereafter, nor forget thy portion in this world: but do thou good, as Allah has been good to thee, and seek not (occasions for) mischief in the land: for Allah loves not those who do mischief." 28:77

Eternity

Life is balanced between this world and the hereafter. Awareness of your intentions and actions, and responsibility for all situations, are necessary for a balance between humanity and divinity.

يَوْمَ تَجِدُ كُلُّ نَفْسٍ مَا عَمِلَتْ مِنْ خَيْرٍ مُحْضَرًا وَمَا عَمِلَتْ مِنْ سُوءٍ تَوَدُّ لَوْ أَنَّ بَيْنَهَا وَبَيْنَهُ أَمَدًا بَعِيدًا ۗ وَيُحَذِّرُكُمُ اللَّهُ نَفْسَهُ ۗ وَاللَّهُ رَءُوفٌ بِالْعِبَادِ 3:30

"On the Day when every soul will be confronted with all the good it has done, and all the evil it has done, it will wish there were a great distance between it and its evil. But Allah cautions you (To remember) Himself. And Allah is full of kindness to those that serve Him." 3:30

Eternity

Every intention and action will have its repercussions. If we do not face them or deal with them now, they will be waiting for us in the hereafter.

وَالَّذِينَ هُمْ لِأَمَانَاتِهِمْ وَعَهْدِهِمْ رَاعُونَ

وَالَّذِينَ هُمْ عَلَىٰ صَلَوَاتِهِمْ يُحَافِظُونَ

أُولَٰئِكَ هُمُ الْوَارِثُونَ

الَّذِينَ يَرِثُونَ الْفِرْدَوْسَ هُمْ فِيهَا خَالِدُونَ 23:8-11

Those who faithfully observe their trusts and their covenants;

And who (strictly) guard their prayers;-

These will be the heirs,

Who will inherit Paradise: they will dwell therein (for ever). 23:8-11

Eternity

To know the One, each one of us needs to be integrated and balanced within ourselves. By being aware and consistent all the time, you sublimate towards cosmic light and thereby experience perpetuity of perfection – paradise at heart.

مَنْ عَمِلَ صَالِحًا مِنْ ذَكَرٍ أَوْ أُنْثَىٰ وَهُوَ مُؤْمِنٌ فَلَنُحْيِيَنَّهُ حَيَاةً طَيِّبَةً ۖ وَلَنَجْزِيَنَّهُمْ أَجْرَهُمْ بِأَحْسَنِ مَا كَانُوا يَعْمَلُونَ 16:97

Whoever works righteousness, man or woman, and has Faith, verily, to him will We give a new Life, a life that is good and pure and We will bestow on such their reward according to the best of their actions. 16:97

Eternity

One step towards truth propels us and is magnified. These steps lead to an awakening to timelessness, to life beyond time.

$$\text{يَا قَوْمِ إِنَّمَا هَٰذِهِ الْحَيَاةُ الدُّنْيَا مَتَاعٌ وَإِنَّ الْآخِرَةَ هِيَ دَارُ الْقَرَارِ} \quad 40:39$$

"O my people! This life of the present is nothing but (temporary) convenience: It is the Hereafter that is the Home that will last. 40:39

Eternity

Our earthly journey is a short prelude to the hereafter's perpetuity. The provisions we need to take on this journey are awareness, adoration and worship of the One.

يَوْمَ تَشْهَدُ عَلَيْهِمْ أَلْسِنَتُهُمْ وَأَيْدِيهِمْ وَأَرْجُلُهُم بِمَا كَانُوا يَعْمَلُونَ 24:24

On the Day when their tongues, their hands, and their feet will bear witness against them as to their actions. 24:24

Eternity

Whatever exists, discloses its nature and on the day of reckoning, every cell will declare its experiences.

أَلَا إِنَّ أَوْلِيَاءَ اللَّهِ لَا خَوْفٌ عَلَيْهِمْ وَلَا هُمْ يَحْزَنُونَ

10:62

Behold! verily on the friends of Allah there is no fear, nor shall they grieve; 10:62

Eternity

Fear and hope are like our two legs, and to be a lover of truth is to transcend Earthly emotions to the constancy of the soul's light.

$$\text{يَوْمَ لَا يَنْفَعُ مَالٌ وَلَا بَنُونَ}$$

$$\text{إِلَّا مَنْ أَتَى اللَّهَ بِقَلْبٍ سَلِيمٍ}$$

$$\text{وَأُزْلِفَتِ الْجَنَّةُ لِلْمُتَّقِينَ } 26:88\text{-}90$$

"The Day whereon neither wealth nor sons will avail,

"But only he (will prosper) that brings to Allah a sound heart;

"To the righteous, the Garden will be brought near, 26:88-90

Eternity

The state of the hereafter, or timelessness, is also present now, although we may be distracted from perceiving it. In the hereafter, we are disempowered and all that we have is a purified heart, which is the home of the effulgent soul. Our life on Earth is a preparation for that state and thus, death is a simple demarcation from a temporary life, to one that is permanent.

هُوَ الَّذِي يُصَلِّي عَلَيْكُمْ وَمَلَائِكَتُهُ لِيُخْرِجَكُم مِّنَ الظُّلُمَاتِ إِلَى النُّورِ ۚ وَكَانَ بِالْمُؤْمِنِينَ رَحِيمًا 33:43

He it is Who sends blessings on you, as do
His angels, that He may bring you out from
the depths of Darkness into Light: and He is
Full of Mercy to the Believers. 33:43

Eternity

The meaning and purpose of life is to move from the darkness of the self, to the soul's brilliance. Having less worldly concerns may be a step towards awareness of on-goingness and continuation of life, Allah's perfect light.

Notes

Notes

www.ingramcontent.com/pod-product-compliance
Lightning Source LLC
Chambersburg PA
CBHW071230090426
42736CB00014B/3029